FUN FACT FILE: WOMEN IN HISTORY

# 20 FUN FACTS ABOUT WOMEN IN ANCIENT EGYPT

By Kristen Rajczak

Gareth Stevens
PUBLISHING

T0018228

Please visit our website, www.garethstevens.com. For a free color catalog of all our high-quality books, call toll free 1-800-542-2595 or fax 1-877-542-2596.

Library of Congress Cataloging-in-Publication Data

Rajczak, Kristen.
 20 fun facts about women in ancient Egypt / Kristen Rajczak.
    pages cm. — (Fun fact file : women in history)
 Includes bibliographical references and index.
 ISBN 978-1-4824-2812-4 (pbk.)
 ISBN 978-1-4824-2813-1 (6 pack)
 ISBN 978-1-4824-2814-8 (library binding)
 1.  Women—Egypt—History—Juvenile literature. 2.  Women—Social life and customs—Juvenile literature. 3. Egypt—History—To 640 A.D.—Juvenile literature.  I. Title. II. Title: Twenty fun facts about women in ancient Egypt.
 HQ1137.E3R35 2016
 305.420932—dc23

                              2014047868


First Edition


Published in 2016 by
**Gareth Stevens Publishing**
111 East 14th Street, Suite 349
New York, NY 10003

Copyright © 2016 Gareth Stevens Publishing

Designer: Samantha DeMartin
Editor: Kristen Rajczak

Photo credits: Cover, p. 1 De Agostini/A. Dagli Orti/De Agostini Picture Library/Getty Images; pp. 4, 7, 15 DEA/G. DAGLI ORTI/De Agostini/Getty Images; p. 5 Andrei nacu/Wikimedia Commons; pp. 6, 25 DEA/S. VANNINI/De Agostini/Getty Images; p. 8 De Agostini Picture Library/De Agostini/Getty Images; p. 9 Leemage/Universal Images Group/Getty Images; pp.10, 16 Science & Society Picture Library/SSPL/Getty Images; pp. 11, 14 DEA/G. DAGLI ORTI/De Agostini Picture Library/Getty Images; pp. 12, 22 ewg3D/E+/Getty Images; pp. 13, 18, 19 Werner Forman/Universal Images Group/ Getty Images; p. 17 Print Collector/Hulton Archive/Getty Images; p. 20 De Agostini/C. Sappa/De Agostini Picture Library/Getty Images; p. 21 LTL/Universal Images Group/Getty Images; p. 23 Wolfgang Kaehler/ LightRocket/Getty Images; p. 24 Horem Web/Wikimedia Commons; p. 26 Ägyptischer Maler/Wikimedia Commons; p. 28 Everett Historical/Shutterstock.com; p. 29 Don Carl STEFFEN/Gamma-Rapho/Getty Images.

Printed in the United States of America

CPSIA compliance information: Batch #CS15GS: For further information contact Gareth Stevens, New York, New York at 1-800-542-2595.

# Contents

Words in the glossary appear in **bold** type the first time they are used in the text.

# Women of Egypt

It's common to read about women in history who didn't have many rights. Their fathers or husbands may have owned them. In some places, women weren't allowed to vote or have any say in government—not in ancient Egypt! Women could own land, do business deals, and even hold jobs.

Nonetheless, being a wife and mother was seen as a woman's most important **role**. In ancient Egypt, having children was a sign of success and earned a woman respect.

SYRIA

Mediterranean Sea

Citium

Byblos

Sidon

Tyre

Gaza

Tanis

Avaris

Memphis Heliopolis

SINAI

CANAAN

Ancient Egypt existed from about 3100 BC to 332 BC. This map shows it around 1500 BC.

IBYA

Herakleopolis

EGYPTIAN EMPIRE

ARABIA

Nile

Abydos

THEBES

Aswan

Elephantine

Abu Simbel

Red Sea

KUSH

Napata

5

## FACT 1

**Records say some Egyptian girls were married by age 8.**

It was common for girls to be between 12 and 14 when they got married. Their husband would be a few years older, about 16 to 20. That seems very young by today's standards!

## FACT 2

# An Egyptian bride didn't wear a wedding dress.

In fact, couples didn't have wedding **ceremonies** at all! Once a woman left her parents' house and moved to her husband's, the pair was considered married. Sometimes their families would have a big party to celebrate, though.

# FACT 3

## Egyptian marriages weren't legal.

To ancient Egyptians, marriage was only a social agreement. That was good for women if they wanted to get out of it! Women could leave their husband and return to their parents' home at any time for any reason. They could marry someone else later, too!

Whatever Egyptian women brought to their marriage, including land, remained theirs once they were married.

8

# FACT 4

## A woman who married the pharaoh might not be the only one!

The pharaoh, or king, of Egypt commonly had many wives. One was the chief wife, and then he'd have lesser wives. Any of the wives' sons could become the next king, but the chief wife's son was likely favored.

## FACT 5

**When expecting a baby, ancient Egyptian women wore a special necklace.**

Women believed wearing amulets, or necklaces, honoring the goddess Taweret brought them a safe childbirth. Taweret had a hippo's head and body, crocodile's tail, and lioness's legs. These animals are known to be very **protective** of their young.

Taweret

Common women often had a lot of children. This was partly because they needed the extra help with their work!

# Some Egyptian women hired nannies.

In ancient Egypt, it was a woman's main job to care for her children and household. If a woman had a job, such as a **priestess**, she'd need someone to watch her children. This was more common in higher social classes.

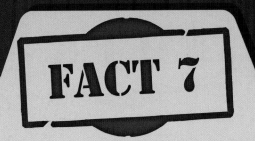

## Egyptian girls likely didn't go to school—even though boys did.

No proof has been found that girls were taught to read and write. It wouldn't have been a big deal, however—only about 2 percent of Egyptians could! Some Egyptian art does show women reading, though.

## An ancient Egyptian woman could stand in for her husband in a business deal.

Egyptian men had great trust in and respect for their wife. In addition to cooking, cleaning, and taking care of children, Egyptian women managed property and worked on their family farm when needed.

In many ways, men and women were equal in ancient Egypt.

# Egyptian Style

## The quality of clothing a woman wore showed her social position.

Egyptians wore clothes made out of a type of cloth called linen. The finer the linen, the wealthier the wearer likely was. Women of high social class also added colors, fancy stitching, and beads to their dresses.

**Ancient Egyptian women wore makeup like colored eye shadow and lipstick.**

**Minerals** were ground and mixed with animal fat to make a paste that was used for makeup. Of course, mostly upper-class women had the time and money to have their makeup done.

Both men and women in ancient Egypt wore black eye makeup. It kept the sun from shining too brightly in their eyes.

# Women of all social classes went to the hairdresser.

Art from ancient Egypt shows women getting their hair done. Combs and hairpins were kept in specially decorated cases. However, wigs were quite popular, so the hair that was being styled may not have been a woman's own!

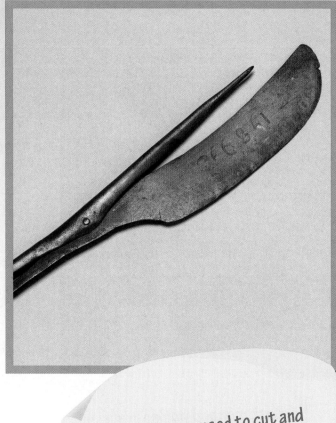

This item was used to cut and curl hair about 3,000 years ago!

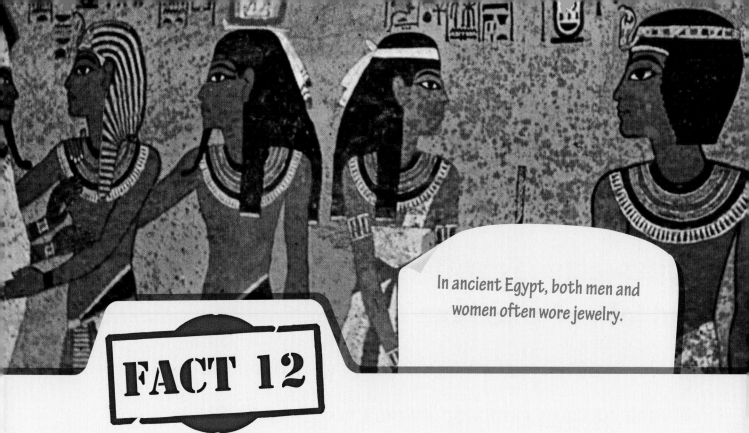

In ancient Egypt, both men and women often wore jewelry.

## FACT 12

## Egyptian women wore earrings, necklaces, and other jewelry made of gold.

Just like today, jewelry was used as the finishing touches of an outfit. Some, like the Taweret amulet, had meaning. Other pieces were to show wealth and style. When parents died, daughters **inherited** their jewelry.

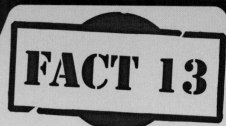

**FACT 13**

## Upper-class Egyptian women had lots of free time.

In wealthy Egyptian homes, the "lady of the house" had servants to cook, clean, and watch her children. So, she was able to to listen to music, enjoy good meals, and travel. She also went to parties, played board games, or simply walked around her gardens.

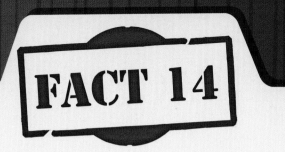
Upper-class Egyptian women often learned how to play music and sing and would even perform at times.

## Ancient Egyptian women rose to the highest levels of government.

Some women served as high officials called stewards, and at least two became prime minister—which was an even higher position! This meant that they might advise the pharaoh on important matters and have an effect on all Egypt.

## Egypt's pharaohs were sometimes women in disguise!

Several women ruled for a time during the history of ancient Egypt. Sobeknefru wore women's clothing, but added some commonly male items to her dress to show she was king. When Hatshepsut ruled Egypt, she was even shown in art wearing a beard!

# An Egyptian queen would often rule for her young son.

A regent is a person who rules in place of someone else. If a child inherited the throne, he wouldn't know what to do! So, his mother could become regent and run things until he was old enough.

Nefertiti was an Egyptian queen who may have ruled Egypt alone after her husband died in 1336 BC.

# Female Rulers of Ancient Egypt

| name | dates of rule | ruled |
| --- | --- | --- |
| Neithikret | 2148–2144 BC | alone |
| Sobeknefru | 1787–1782 BC | alone |
| Hatshepsut | 1473–1458 BC | alone |
| Nefertiti | 1352–1336 BC | with her husband Akhenaten |
| Twosret | 1187–1185 BC | alone |
| Cleopatra VII | 51–30 BC | with her brothers Ptolemy XII and Ptolemy XIII and her son Ptolemy XV Caesar |

Regents could be the mother, sister, or wife of a king unable to rule for some reason. They might also be coregent with a son, brother, or husband.

Egyptian queens had household duties, too! They were expected to help their husband with leaders from other kingdoms and generally strengthen the royal family's position in Egypt.

## FACT 17

## Ancient Egyptian queens were considered almost gods.

Though they didn't hold all the kingdom's power, Egyptian queens had a lot of power over their own life. They had land, built monuments if they wanted to, and were often **worshiped!**

## FACT 18

Only a very important woman would have a tomb next to King Menkaure, one of the pharaohs buried in the Pyramids of Giza.

## Queen Khentkawes is buried near the Pyramids of Giza.

The three most famous pyramids in Egypt were built as **tombs** for kings. But there's another tomb—built next to the smallest Pyramid—for Khentkawes. She may have been King Menkaure's daughter.

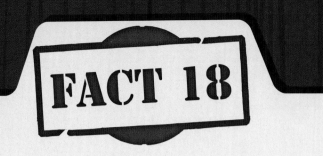

## Egypt's last ruler was a woman.

During much of Cleopatra's rule, the Roman Empire wanted to take over Egypt. She tried to stop it by befriending Roman leaders, but it didn't help her in the end. She died in 30 BC as Roman armies prepared to take her kingdom.

Though Cleopatra ruled Egypt, she wasn't Egyptian. She was Greek!

## FACT 20

**Egyptians worshiped female goddesses throughout their history.**

Some of the largest temples in Egypt were built to honor goddesses such as Bastet. The Egyptians believed it was just as important to worship them as the male gods.

Isis

Each goddess was believed to have a job, including protecting people or crops. Page 27 shows some of the goddesses of the ancient Egyptians and why they were worshiped.

# Who to Worship?

**Nephthys**
protector of the dead

**Bastet**
goddess of the home, fire, and cats

**Taweret**
goddess of childbirth

**Hathor**
goddess of love, protector of women

**Isis**
goddess of Earth, rebirth, and destruction

**Sekhmet**
goddess of war

Following the fall of ancient Egypt, women lost many of their rights. They had to obey the laws of the Roman Empire, which meant their father or husband was in charge of the decisions of the household. Marriages were commonly arranged.

It took thousands of years to return to the equality women had in Egypt. In fact, many rights women have today in countries like the United States have only been granted in the last 100 years!

Women all over the world still fight to have rights similar to those Egyptian women had thousands of years ago!

**ceremony:** an event to honor or celebrate something

**disguise:** the state of having a false appearance

**inherit:** to get by legal right after a person's death

**jewelry:** pieces of metal, often holding gems, worn on the body

**legal:** having to do with the law

**mineral:** matter in the ground that forms rocks

**priestess:** a woman who performs religious ceremonies

**protective:** keeping safe

**quality:** the standard or grade of something

**role:** a social position

**tomb:** a burial room

**worship:** to honor as a god

# For More Information

## Books

Napoli, Donna Jo. *Treasury of Egyptian Mythology: Classic Stories of Gods, Goddesses, Monsters & Mortals.* Washington, DC: National Geographic, 2013.

Rockwood, Leigh. *Ancient Egyptian Daily Life.* New York, NY: PowerKids Press, 2014.

Twist, Clint. *Cleopatra: Queen of Egypt.* Somerville, MA: Candlewick Press, 2012.

## Websites

**Ancient Egypt Daily Life**
*www.kidsgen.com/ancient_egypt/daily_life.htm*
Read more about the daily life of an ancient Egyptian.

**Ten Facts About Ancient Egypt!**
*www.ngkids.co.uk/did-you-know/Ten-Facts-about-Ancient-Egypt*
Find out lots more about ancient Egypt.

# Index